Jane Burton

Badger at Home

story by
Shirley Greenway

M

PAN MACMILLAN CHILDREN'S BOOKS

For Olivia, Francesca and Alessandro
from SG

For Lilian, who gave me Patch
from JB

A TRELD BICKNELL BOOK

Photographs copyright © 1992 by Jane Burton
Text copyright © 1992 by Shirley Greenway

First published in this edition 1993 by
PAN MACMILLAN CHILDREN'S BOOKS
A division of Pan Macmillan Limited
London and Basingstoke
Associated companies throughout the world

This Picturemac edition published 1993

ISBN 0-333-59252-2

Typeset in Bembo by Chambers Wallace
Printed in Hong Kong

A little animal lies at the foot of a cliff
where he had fallen in the night.
His dark fur stands out
against the chalky ground.
His body is hurt and cold,
and very very still.
He is a baby badger, just alive.

He is seen by children out walking.
Gently they lift him and hear
a faint little sound: *Cr-e-e-e-a-ak.*

The children carry him safely home.
They live in an old schoolhouse
where wounded animals often come.
For three days they carefully tend him.
He is warmed and fed and protected.
"Poor badger," they say. "Poor old badger."
And so, Badger he became,
with no other name.

Badger is timid and shy,
but he knows that he is safe.
He listens with his sensitive ears,
and savours new smells with his quick nose.

But his short-sighted eyes find
the daylight bright and strange.
Badger drinks greedily from his bottle.
He begins to be healthy and strong.

Soon, milk is not enough
to feed this hungry little animal.
He guzzles meaty food
from a big red bowl.
Chomp, chomp, chomp!
Badger makes a lot of noise
and even more mess.
He rakes the food with his long claws
and leaves meaty footprints all around.
Badger grows bigger and stronger.
He explores the sounds and smells
of the rambling schoolhouse.
He is a daytime, indoor sort of badger . . .

Badger is *very* friendly and playful,
but he has no brother badgers to play with.
Instead he has a soft toy badger.
It is black and white and silver –
just like him.
He marks his toy with his own special scent.
Now it belongs only to him.

The garden is big and unfamiliar.

Badger is afraid to go out of doors.

But he likes to follow the friendly legs

of his new family.

One day he follows the legs into the garden.

It smells very strange – all green and flowery.

But Badger doesn't explore

and he doesn't dig.

Timid Badger stays right where he is.

Vr-r-r-o-o-o-m-m!

An aeroplane booms across the sky.

Poor Badger, he won't let go until

he is safely back indoors.

Badger makes himself "at home".
He is very neat and tidy,
carefully cleaning his sleek, silvery fur.
Each night, Badger chooses
a new spot for his bed.
He drags his favourite rug –
an old sheepskin coat –
into a comfortable place.

Three new puppies come to the schoolhouse.

Sammy and Suzie and Patch.

They are waiting to go to their new homes.

Sammy and Suzie are golden,

pretty and clever.

Patch is very odd-looking.

He has a patch over one eye

and a coat of black and white.

One eye is brown and the other bright blue . . .

Patch is good and gentle
and tries to be brave.
But it is hard for him,
because he is deaf and cannot hear.
Sammy and Suzie always tease Patch
and make him give up his bones.

Sammy and Suzie *always* make mischief.
They crowd into Patch's basket
with all the toys.
Suzie steals Badger's favourite toy,
and pulls out its stuffing.
This makes Badger cross.
Suzie runs away when Badger comes,
but Sammy isn't afraid of anything.
Badger is very strong –
even stronger than Sammy.
They roll over and over on the floor.
The puppy never gives in.

At last, Sammy and Suzie go to new homes.
There is *no* new home for Patch.
No-one wants a puppy who cannot hear
with a dog's special ears.
So Patch is left alone with Badger,
the wild animal who won't leave the house.

But Badger isn't bossy like Sammy,
and Patch doesn't steal like Suzie.
Patch joins Badger for a good meal.
He eats until his tummy is full.
Then – *lick, lick, lick* – greedy
Badger cleans the bowl.

Patch is happy now.

His brother and sister have gone away.

Badger is happy, too. *Ninger-ninger-ning.*

He gives his contented chuckle.

Now he has a playmate of his own size.

Together they choose new places to sleep
and curl up together at night.

Those two naughty puppies can't steal it,
so Badger lets Patch play
with his favourite toy.

Soon its stuffing is ALL gone!

Badger finds a shoe.

He likes its strong leathery smell.

He licks it and chews it

and drags it along with him.

It is a good game. Patch wants to join in.

He pulls on a shoelace. But, when he tries

to pull the shoe towards *him*,

his paw gets in the way of Badger's teeth.

Ye-e-l-l-p! Patch looks surprised, but he knows

that Badger doesn't mean to hurt him.

Badger isn't bossy and spiteful, like Sammy.

One day Badger and Patch find a broom
leaning against the wall.
The bristles are fun to chew and claw.
They shake it back and forth.
Cr-a-a-a-a-a-s-s-s-h!
The broom handle hits the floor.
Badger jumps and runs away in fright,
but Patch goes right on chewing.
He hasn't heard a thing.
Soon Badger calms down and
comes back to claw some more.

Patch and Badger are always together.

They make a good pair.

They share their food, toys and baskets.

They chase and bite and tumble and argue –
but always make it up again.

After all, what are friends for?

Because he can't hear
the cars whizzing by,
Patch is not allowed
to go near the road.
But Badger will go
wherever Patch goes.
It is time to explore.
Badger follows Patch
out into the field.
He is still timid,
but Patch feels brave
and likes adventures.
They come to the pond.

Badger can't see
the dark water
under the leaves.
Patch can't hear it
gurgling. *Sn-n-i-i-ff!*
They test it with their noses.
The pond smells interesting.
The weed looks like grass.
In goes Patch. *Br-r-r-r-r!*
Badger doesn't dare.
The "grass" is wet and cold.
Patch clambers out.
Let's go somewhere else!

The two friends stay together –
and together they are still.
Badger lends Patch his ears,
while Patch has sharp eyes
and courage enough for both.
They keep each other safe
in the big world outside.
But most of all they like being at home
in the old schoolhouse.
Just a happy household badger – and friend.